MW00898038

This book belongs to

_____

COLORS,
SHAPES,
AND SIZES

A Bantam  Book

BANTAM BOOKS
TORONTO • NEW YORK • LONDON • SYDNEY • AUCKLAND

COLORS, SHAPES, AND SIZES
A Bantam Book / October 1985

Adapted from the Walt Disney Fun-to-Learn Library:
Adventures in Colors and Shapes *(volume 3) and*
Big and Little, Same and Different *(volume 4).*

Library of Congress Catalog Card Number: 85-43077

All rights reserved.
Copyright © 1985 by Walt Disney Productions.
This book may not be reproduced in whole or in part, by
mimeograph or any other means, without permission.
For information address: Walt Disney Productions,
500 South Buena Vista Street, Burbank, CA 91521.

ISBN 0-553-05534-8

Published simultaneously in the United States and Canada

Bantam Books are published by Bantam Books, Inc. Its trade-
mark, consisting of the words "Bantam Books" and the por-
trayal of a rooster, is Registered in U.S. Patent and Trademark
Office and in other countries. Marca Registrada. Bantam
Books, Inc., 666 Fifth Avenue, New York, New York 10103.

PRINTED IN THE UNITED STATES OF AMERICA

DW   0 9 8 7 6 5 4 3 2 1

ADVENTURES IN
COLORS AND SHAPES

blue

The world is full of color, everywhere we look. Many people like one color best of all.

Cinderella's favorite color is blue. Here she is in her blue dress, dancing with Prince Charming.

"I like blue, too," says the Blue Fairy. "When I wave my wand, I can make everything turn blue!"

Look! Pooh is painting the house blue—and Eeyore, too!

red

Winnie-the-Pooh sings a happy song
as he floats through the air:
"I like red la-la-la,
Overhead la-la-la,
And I hope you will note
I am wearing a coat
That's as red as red can be."

Captain Hook looks very surprised. He's found a big red fish—and he wasn't even trying! Captain Hook's favorite color is red.

yellow

Rabbit says yellow is his favorite color. Maybe that's because he is yellow himself. When he invites his friends for tea, he bakes a beautiful yellow cake and puts yellow frosting on it. Eeyore finds Pooh's present of yellow flowers quite delicious.

Alice finds a whole garden of yellow flowers in Wonderland. The yellow bread-and-butterflies come to say good morning. Alice thinks they are flowers that have learned to fly.

green

Robin Hood and his Merry Men are in the green forest—the place they like best of all. They have a big green sack full of money to give to poor people. It's so heavy, Friar Tuck can hardly lift it.

"Hurrah!" Peter Pan cheers, as the great green crocodile swims past him, chasing wicked Captain Hook.

gray

Little gray Dumbo is happy when he's flying over the circus parade. Here comes big gray Mrs. Jumbo, thump-thumping round the ring.

"Help!" shouts their clown friend. "I think I'd rather walk!"

orange

Look out! Here comes the great orange tiger, Shere Khan. He's really fierce, but Mowgli's not afraid.
Even the monkeys are laughing at the big Shere Khan.

pink and purple

Geppetto the wood-carver likes to make toys. Today he has made a toy castle, and he is painting it pink. It will make a lovely home for the pink princess doll.

Geppetto has made a toy elephant in a purple coat, and he has made other purple toys, too. He has made a purple duck and a purple wagon for Figaro.

Bambi is very proud when he meets his handsome brown father in the forest. "Whoo! Whoo!" the brown owl calls to Bambi.

brown

The big brown ape-king is happiest when he's eating. Today his little brown monkey friends bring him fruit for his dinner.

black and white

When Lucky Puppy and his brothers and sisters play together, there are white coats and black spots everywhere. Now they are having a tug-of-war. The prize is a big black boot.

Flower the skunk sees himself in a forest pond. "Oh, my!" he says happily. "I never knew I was so handsome. No one else in the forest has a more beautiful coat than mine."

"Happy Halloween, everybody!" says
Clarabelle Cow. She is dressed in a black
witch-costume for her party. Mickey Mouse is
the white ghost. "Boo!" he says.

Clarabelle Cow sees other colors at her
party. Minnie is wearing an orange tutu. The
jack-o'-lantern is also orange. The kittens are
gray. And Clarabelle's shoes are brown.

circle

Timothy Mouse is happiest when he's at the circus. Today he's looking for circles there.

He finds an elephant riding a funny bicycle.

He finds a clown
holding a hoop for his dog,

a balloon man selling
colorful round balloons,

and a seal balancing
something big and round
on his nose.

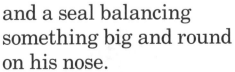

Huey, Dewey, and Louie are having a great time in their wonderful playroom. Everywhere they look, they see things that are square.

square

They see a toybox with square sides, filled to the top with toys.

They see a jack-in-the-box
with square sides. It makes
Huey jump.

Dewey uses blocks to
build a big square wall.

Huey, Dewey, and Louie laugh
at a funny square picture.
It is Uncle Scrooge as a baby!

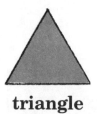

triangle

Triangles are everywhere in Hiawatha's village. There is even a triangle at the end of Hiawatha's arrow. Something else is there, too.

"Go away!" Hiawatha shouts. "You are spoiling my aim!"

Sunflower is busy weaving a surprise for Hiawatha. It's a blanket covered with orange and yellow triangles. There are more triangles in Sunflower's headband. Even the tents look like triangles.

Uncle Scrooge is happiest when he is showing his family how rich he is. There are many rectangles in his treasure room.

rectangle

These gold bars have rectangle-shaped sides. Huey, Dewey, and Louie use the bars to build a fort.

"Catch!" shouts Uncle Scrooge. He throws money into the air. His money is also shaped like rectangles.

This safe is shaped like a rectangle, too. It is full of jewels, and Uncle Scrooge lets Daisy wear them.

Mickey Mouse is proud and happy when he leads the marching band. There are shapes everywhere in his parade—a big square, some small rectangles, some circles, and lots of triangles.

oval

diamond

"The world is full of different shapes," says Jiminy Cricket. He sees ovals and diamonds.

The oval reminds Snow White's stepmother of her magic mirror. Once upon a time it told her she was the fairest in the land.

Pooh's kite is the shape of a diamond. Hang on, Piglet! This diamond is going up into the sky.

heart

star

Clarabelle Cow says the heart is her favorite shape. She has baked a plate of special heart-shaped cookies for Valentine's Day.

"Make a wish!" says the Blue Fairy. When she waves her magic wand with the star-tip, the wish will come true.

"The best way to end a happy day is with fireworks," Mickey says. "I wish we could see fireworks every night of the year."

Mickey sees a square and a triangle. Minnie sees a circle and a rectangle.

Up in the sky is a whole rainbow of fireworks. Morty and Ferdie know all the colors. They see red and blue, yellow and green, and even pink. They don't have favorite colors. They like every color best of all!

BIG AND LITTLE, SAME AND DIFFERENT

"I love to fly!" shouts Peter Pan. "Flying is the best fun there is!"

Peter is on his way to visit Wendy and John and Michael Darling.

Peter watches for four towers. Three are just the *same*. One is *different*. He knows he must turn when he sees the different one.

On his way Peter had to fly over a park. He knew he had to fly toward one tree that was different from the others.

"I see Wendy's house!" Peter exclaims. "It looks different from the others." Wendy's house is red.

Upstairs in the nursery Wendy, John, and little Michael are busy playing. "Here's how I build a tower," Michael tells Wendy. Two of Michael's towers have the same shape. One has a different shape.

"Look at the Indians in my picture," says John proudly. Three of John's Indians are just the same.

Now John and Michael want to play pirates. John waves his *long* wooden sword. "Clear the decks," he shouts. Michael's sword is *shorter*. The boys knock down Michael's block towers and bump into everything. See what they've done to the nursery!

"Look out!" says Wendy. The *big* rocking chair almost falls over. Nana the dog catches it—just in time. The *smaller* chair belongs to the teddy bear. He's hiding from the sword fight.

"Peter is here!" Wendy runs to
the window to welcome her friend.
Naughty Tinker Bell makes
a face at Wendy.
"*I'm* Peter's friend,"
she thinks.

John and Michael can't wait for their Never Land adventure to begin. They shout hello from their beds. John's bed is the *longest*. Michael's is *middle-sized*. The teddy is tucked into the *shortest* one.

Most of the toys have been put away. But John and Michael forgot the toy boats lying on the floor. The *biggest* boat looks like a pirate ship. That belongs to John. The *smallest* is a rowboat. That is Michael's favorite. The *middle-sized* boat is the blue-and-green one.

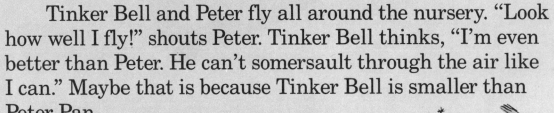

Tinker Bell and Peter fly all around the nursery. "Look how well I fly!" shouts Peter. Tinker Bell thinks, "I'm even better than Peter. He can't somersault through the air like I can." Maybe that is because Tinker Bell is smaller than Peter Pan.

Soon Peter and Tinker Bell will teach Wendy and her brothers how to fly.

Big Nana and the little teddy bear are watching. They might like to fly, too.

As the children are flying around the nursery, in the
far-off Never Land the pirates watch for Peter to come
back. Three of the pirates are the same. One pirate is
different—and he's in trouble. Watch out!

The Indian chief and his friend want to catch fish for their dinner. The *shorter* Indian has hooked something very big. Maybe the chief, who is *taller*, will help him pull it in.

The Indian brave looks at the fish he has caught. It is much shorter than the fish the little Indian caught.

"Today we hunt. Follow me," says the big chief. He is the *tallest* Indian. He is walking in front of a *middle-sized* Indian and the *shortest* Indian.

Three totem poles guard the Indian village. One is very tall. One is very short. And one is middle-sized.

"A fierce animal is coming!" The shortest Indian has climbed up on a stump so that he can look around.

"Run," he shouts. "Run away!"

The tall chief and his friend look for places where they can hide. A tall tree will make a good hiding place for the chief. The shorter tree is just right for the other Indian.

Look at what frightened the Indians. Bunnies!

While the Indians hide, the pirate ship bounces over the waves.

"I'm hungry!" roars fierce Captain Hook. He cuts a *thick* slice of pirate-food cake for his lunch. "I'm hungry, too," says Smee in a soft voice. But Captain Hook doesn't listen. He cuts a *thin* slice for First Mate Smee.

The other pirates are still waiting for their cake. "We'd like thick pieces, too," they say. They have found boards to sit on while they eat their lunch. One board is thick. The other board is thin. Oh, no! The thin board is about to break.

Now Peter and the Darlings are in the Never Land. "Flying is easy," Peter says. "Look at me!" He whizzes *over* the top of an old hollow tree. But Wendy is still learning to fly. She wobbles as she flies *under* a branch.

"*Whoooo!*" cries the sleepy owl. "What noisy person woke me up?"

Up, up John goes into the air. And *down,* down comes Michael. The big bear is surprised when he sees a teddy bear coming down from the sky.

"*Grrr,*" he growls. "It's raining boys and bears!"

Peter wants to show his friends all of the
Never Land. He flies *in front of* Wendy to lead
the way. Tinker Bell comes along *behind* and
watches out for danger.

"Look down there," Peter shouts. "Captain Hook is in trouble." The captain splashes along just in front of the hungry crocodile.

"I'll save you, Captain!" shouts Smee. He is behind the crocodile, and he rows hard to catch up.

"We'd better not get too close to the pirate ship,"
Wendy says. She sees pirates in the crow's nest near
the *top* of the mast, and more pirates at the *bottom*.
One pirate has climbed to the *middle* of the mast.
He's shouting at Peter! But Peter isn't scared of
anything. He swoops in to cut the sails. Once the
sails are gone, the boat will stop moving.

In the underground house under Hangman's Tree, Tinker Bell signals a warning. The pirates are coming to seek their revenge! The boys hurry to the ladder. They are all ready to fight the pirates.

Peter climbs to the top of the ladder. John is on the bottom.

Tinker Bell flies up over the stool, where she can see what's happening. But the teddy bear hides under the stool.

"Ahoy, you pirates!" shouts Peter. "Watch out for me!"
Up he flies, up from the door of the underground house.
The pirates are afraid.

"Help!" shouts one.

"Save me!" shouts another.

"Great skulls and crossbones," says a third. "Let's hide."

They all jump down from Hangman's Tree and
run away.

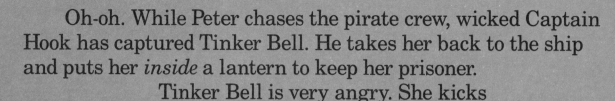

Oh-oh. While Peter chases the pirate crew, wicked Captain
Hook has captured Tinker Bell. He takes her back to the ship
and puts her *inside* a lantern to keep her prisoner.

Tinker Bell is very angry. She kicks
the glass and shakes her fist at Hook.
Hook just laughs, but Smee is afraid. He's
glad he's *outside* the lantern and Tinker
Bell is inside, where she can't reach him.

"When the Lost Boys come to rescue Tinker Bell, I'll capture them, too," roars Hook. "I'll lock them up and never let them out," he promises.

Hook leaves the lantern *on top of* the table. Poor Smee! He shivers and shakes when the captain is angry. He hides *under* the table.

Don't worry, Tinker Bell. The Lost Boys are on their way.

"We'll find Tinker Bell," John says bravely. He is in front, leading the search party. Little Michael and his teddy are behind.

Look! Four of the pirates are hiding along the way. They want to know where the Lost Boys are going. The first pirate hides inside a hollow stump. The second hides behind a tree. The third pirate peers over the top of a rock. The fourth pirate hides behind the bushes.

Guess where Peter is. He's off to find the ship—and Captain Hook.

"Follow me!" John orders. "Forward, march."
He marches right under a waterfall. John's umbrella
keeps him *dry*, but poor Michael gets all *wet*.
The teddy bear gets wet, too!

"Step on the rocks to cross the river," Cubby says. But one rock turns out to be a hippopotamus! Cubby slips off into the water. Now he is wet, too.

At last the Lost Boys reach the pirate ship, and Peter zooms down from the sky.

"Away you go, Captain Hook," shouts Peter. He pushes the captain right off the rigging. Smack! Hook falls on the deck. It is very *hard*. Another boy pushes Smee across the deck. But Smee is luckier than the captain. The place he lands on is *soft*.

"Here's Tinker Bell," shouts John. He has rescued her from the ship's cabin. All the Lost Boys cheer as they fight the pirates.

The battle is over at last. Captain Hook is very sore
and tired. He soaks his feet in a tub of *hot* water. Smee
holds a piece of ice to soothe the captain's poor aching
head. It feels nice and *cold*.

"Get me a pillow," the captain moans. A pirate
brings a soft pillow for the captain. "Get me a thick slice
of cake," the captain roars. Another pirate brings him a
thick slice of cake to make him feel better.

The pirate with the pillow is the tallest. The pirate
who brought the cake is the smallest. Smee is middle-sized.

Everyone is happy because Tinker Bell is safe. The
Lost Boys have a party, with all kinds of good things to
eat and drink. Peter and John have a make-believe fight.
"Here's how we beat the pirates!" shouts Peter.

The boys are hungry and thirsty. Two are eating
thick, juicy sandwiches. Two are drinking hot cocoa.
Another is drinking cold lemonade.

Two of the boys sit on soft pillows on the bed. One is
sitting on a stool. It feels very hard.

After the party Wendy goes for a walk beside the lagoon. "The water is so *smooth,* I can see myself in it," she says. Little fish come to look at the pretty girl at the edge of the lagoon.

Splash! Naughty Tinker Bell swoops down and hits the water. Now the surface is *rough.* Wendy can't see herself anymore. And Tinker Bell has frightened the fish!

"Whee!" the Lost Boys shout. They are having fun sliding down a hill. The slope is grassy and smooth. They slide fast.

"Ouch," groans Cubby. He slides off the grass and onto some rocks. His slide is slow—and rough!

Peter wants to play a trick on the captain. He has three helpers with him.

John is the biggest one. Michael is the middle-sized one. And Tinker Bell is the smallest helper.

"Where is that Peter Pan?" Hook wonders. The captain kneels on a smooth, dry rock and looks through his spyglass. But he can't find Peter!

"One, two, three. BOO!" Peter and his helpers scare Captain Hook right into the water. The captain is surprised—and very angry. He lands on some rough rocks and gets all wet.

"Peter Pan has beaten me this time," thinks Hook. "But someday, I'll catch him."

Now the adventure is over, and Wendy, John, and Michael are home again. "Good-bye, Peter. Good-bye, Tinker Bell." They wave to their friends.

Nana is glad the children are home. She falls asleep under the table. Michael's teddy bear rests on top of the table.

All night long Wendy, John, and Michael will remember their adventures in the Never Land. And all night long they will think about the wonderful things they will do when Peter comes again.

Pleasant dreams!

POPCORN PANCAKES

PEANUTS

WELCOME